What if we do NOthing?

DRUG TRAFFICKING

Nathaniel Harris

W
FRANKLIN WATTS
LONDON•SYDNEY

First published in 2009 by Franklin Watts

Copyright © 2009 Arcturus Publishing Limited

Franklin Watts
338 Euston Road
London NW1 3BH

Franklin Watts Australia
Level 17/207 Kent Street, Sydney, NSW 2000

Produced by Arcturus Publishing Limited,
26/27 Bickels Yard, 151-153 Bermondsey Street,
London SE1 3HA

The right of Nathaniel Harris to be identified as
the author of this work has been asserted by
him in accordance with the Copyright, Designs
and Patents Act 1988.

Series concept: Alex Woolf
Editor: Alex Woolf
Designer: Phipps Design
Picture researcher: Alex Woolf

A CIP catalogue record for this book is available
from the British Library.

Dewey Decimal Classification Number: 363.45

ISBN 978 0 7496 8747 2

Printed in China

Franklin Watts is a division of Hachette
Children's Books, an Hachette UK company.
www.hachette.co.uk

Picture Credits
Corbis: cover *bottom left* (Bob Thomas), cover *top right* (Reuters),
5 (Bob Thomas), 6 (Scott Houston/Sygma), 9 (Ed Kashi), 13
(Reuters), 14 (John and Lisa Merrill), 16 (Andy Clark/Reuters), 24
(Oswaldo Rivas/Reuters), 28 (Gideon Mendel for The International
HIV/AIDS Alliance), 31 (Bettmann), 35 (Adrees Latif/Reuters), 36
(Reuters), 39 (Damir Sagolj/Reuters), 40 (David Bathgate), 42
(Reuters), 44 (Scott Houston).
Getty Images: 10 (Paula Bronstein), 21 (Robert Nickelsberg), 22
(Rodrigo Arangua/AFP), 33 (Santi Visalli Inc).
PA Photos: 17 (AP).
Rex Features: 18 (Sam Foot).
Science Photo Library: 27 (CC Studio).
Shutterstock: cover *background* (Ricardo A Alves).

Cover pictures
bottom left: A young drug addict sits on the floor of a public toilet.
top right: Pakistani anti-narcotics police display bags of heroin and
morphine seized from Iranian drug smugglers in Turbat, near the
Iranian border, in January 2002.
background: A poppy field. Opium, as well as opiates such as
morphine and heroin, are processed from the sap of the opium
poppy.

Every attempt has been made to clear copyright. Should there be
any inadvertent omission, please apply to the publisher for
rectification.

Contents

CHAPTER 1

The Trouble with Drugs

It is 2025. Tom and his friends occupy a broken-down old house that they don't clean or decorate. In fact, Tom and his friends don't do much of anything. Mostly they talk about drugs and how to get hold of them. 'No problem,' says Tom. 'There are dealers everywhere. You can buy as much as you want. The problem is finding the money for them.' That's hard, especially when you need more and more drugs just to stop feeling bad. The friends talk about Julie, a girl who has died from a drug overdose. Tom looks round at his friends. They aren't in good shape, and neither is he. Then another friend turns up with some drugs. There is just about enough to go round. One after another, the friends inject the drug into their veins. Soon, for a little while, they will be 'high' and won't care what happens to them.

Victims of a global trade

The future doesn't look good for these young drug addicts. Illegal drug use is already spoiling their lives. Even if you think that is their own fault, they need help. If they want to stop, they will find it hard because there are people who will sell them drugs. Even now, well before 2025, producing and supplying illegal drugs is big business. 'Trafficking' means illegal trading, and drug trafficking is a criminal activity on an international scale. It involves many thousands of people.

This diagram shows estimated world drug use among people in the age group 15-64. The total age group numbers around 4,117 million. Of these, around 200 million use drugs. Problem drug users (defined by the United Nations as people who inject a drug or make regular or long-term use of opium-based drugs, cocaine or amphetamines) number around 25 million.

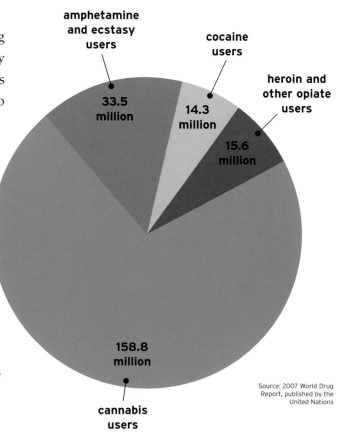

amphetamine and ecstasy users
33.5 million

cocaine users
14.3 million

heroin and other opiate users
15.6 million

cannabis users
158.8 million

Source: 2007 World Drug Report, published by the United Nations

What are drugs?

A drug is a chemical substance that has a physical or mental effect. It influences the way people feel or think, or the way their bodies work. When we talk about 'drugs' as a problem or menace, we are actually talking about illegal drugs, also called narcotics. We often use 'drugs' as shorthand for 'illegal drugs', but we should remember that there are legal as well as illegal drugs. Medicines are drugs. In fact, some illegal drugs were originally developed as medicines. They were only outlawed, or issued under strictly controlled conditions, when experts realized that they might be abused. Other, non-medicinal drugs are legally sold and used every day. These include alcohol, the nicotine in tobacco and the caffeine in coffee, tea and soft drinks.

Down and out. This young addict has lost almost everything. He is homeless and has nothing much left except some drug-taking gear and a mattress. Not every drug taker ends up like this, but the drugs path is a dangerous one to take.

Types of drug

Drugs can be divided into groups. Each group has widely different effects. One group consists of stimulants. These energizing drugs make the heart rate speed up and thoughts race through the mind. People who have taken stimulants may act strangely, grinding their teeth. In some cases they suffer from serious mental disorders. Stimulants include cocaine, amphetamines, crystal meth (methamphetamine) and ecstasy.

Another group, called sedatives, or depressants, have the opposite effect. They slow the heartbeat and the functioning of the brain. Users feel sensations of numbness, drowsiness and lack of

Clubbing. A young man has a good time at a New York club, showing off his skill with glow sticks. In the 1990s ecstasy became the clubber's drug of choice, energizing users so that they could dance the night away.

6

coordination (ability to make the limbs work together). Opium, heroin and most forms of cannabis (marijuana) are sedative drugs.

The third group consists of hallucinogens. These are drugs that make the users hallucinate, which means that they experience reality in an abnormal way. The drug taker may see everything in intensely vivid colours or mistake imaginary things for realities. A commonly used hallucinogen is the synthetic (human-made) drug LSD. Another is 'magic mushrooms', which describes two species of wild mushrooms, liberty cap and fly agaric.

Drug dangers

Drugs interfere dramatically with the way the mind and body work, so it is no great surprise that there are big downsides to drug use. One risk is that drug users might take an overdose – a dangerously large amount of a drug. An overdose is almost always very serious, and sometimes fatal. It can happen because the drug user is careless or badly informed. It can also happen because the ingredients of illegal substances have never been officially checked and are dangerous. For example, the proportions may be wrong. Pure heroin and pure cocaine are killers – they need to be mixed with other substances. Sometimes the substances added to a drug may also prove to be health hazards.

LEGAL BUT LETHAL

In most societies, adults can legally buy and use alcohol and tobacco. For a long time, these drugs were seen as a normal part of life. Many people still think of them in that way. Yet alcohol abuse ruins lives and causes illness and death. In the United Kingdom the cost of alcohol abuse in terms of medical treatment, policing and lost working days was estimated in 2003 at almost £20 billion. The links between smoking and diseases such as cancer are well established. Smoking has declined in the United States, yet smoking-related healthcare and other costs were estimated at US$167 billion in 2005.

Drug taking has many other hazards. Just as drugs differ from one another, so do their drawbacks. Side effects and after effects can include sweating, a dry mouth, vomiting, constipation and diarrhoea. More unpleasant things can happen while the user is under the influence of the drug. Some people suffer panic attacks. Hallucinogenic drugs can cause a 'bad trip' in which the user experiences imaginary horrors and may behave irrationally. The Netherlands is generally less tough on drugs than most of its European neighbours, but in 2007 it banned the sale of hallucinogenic mushrooms after users behaved strangely or violently. In one incident a girl died.

(opposite) Paying the price. This woman in a San Francisco county hospital is suffering agonies. She is not ill in the ordinary sense of the word, but her body craves the drug she has become addicted to and cannot have.

Addiction

One major problem with many drugs is that highs are followed by lows. When the effect of the drug wears off, the user is often left feeling tired, depressed or irritable. He or she may well take the drug again in order to feel better. This is one way in which people slip from occasional drug use into addiction (also known as dependence). Addicts are people who need to take a drug frequently and cannot stop, even when they realize it is spoiling their lives.

Many drugs are addictive to a greater or lesser extent. Users of a drug such as heroin eventually need it as a relief rather than a pleasure. They suffer from terrible pains when they cannot get it or are trying to give it up. Some other drugs are described as psychologically addictive. They cause addiction through their influence on the mind. To stop taking them may not be physically uncomfortable, but the user's brain craves the release given by the drug and the way it blots out other problems and anxieties in their life.

HEROIN

Heroin is generally regarded as the most dangerous of all illegal drugs. It is an opiate - one of a range of drugs made from the opium poppy, including opium, morphine and codeine. Heroin was originally developed around 1900 as an exceptionally powerful painkiller. Illegally sold in powder form, it can be sniffed or smoked. Many users dissolve the powder in water and inject it into a vein to achieve a rapid 'rush'. It is highly addictive and causes a number of ailments. It also carries more serious health risks from overdosing, collapsed veins and diseases caught through sharing needles.

Addicts end up taking large amounts of their drug. Their systems get used to it, and they need more and more to achieve the same effect. Even if they can afford to buy large quantities, addicts find that the drug dominates their lives and prevents them from having normal relationships. Furthermore, taking large quantities of a drug makes its long-term effects worse. In some instances, the long-term user suffers serious mental problems or a failure of the heart or liver. Regular snorting of cocaine has a particularly unattractive effect: it destroys the snorter's septum, the partition separating the nostrils.

Glue sniffing. A boy inhales glue from a bag on the streets of Kathmandu in Nepal. Very young children in many countries find it easy to get hold of everyday products like glue that can be used as drugs.

Those who take more than one type of drug at a time are even more likely to develop serious problems.

What type of people take drugs?

Despite the risks, people all over the world use drugs. The drug taker is often portrayed as a young person, because the young are often rebellious and like to take risks. Young people also sometimes find it hard to resist peer pressure – the pressure to behave like other young people they know.

Anti-drugs campaigners understandably target the young, hoping to prevent them from starting a drug habit. But millions of adults are also users. They belong to all sorts of groups, ranging from cocaine-snorting businesspeople and partygoers to poor people, who take drugs to forget their troubles for a time. Sports enthusiasts sometimes use drugs called steroids, not to change how they feel but to build up muscles and improve performance.

Not all drug users are supplied by dealers. Some adults who use prescription drugs become addicted to them. And many children get hold of legally available solvents, such as glue and lighter fuel, and get a high from sniffing them.

People have used drugs for thousands of years. But in modern times, mass production, rapid communications and international transportation have made large quantities of drugs available all over the world.

Sending out a message

Research has identified many of the dangers of drug taking, but many people – including smokers and drinkers – ignore the message. Governments see it as their duty to protect citizens and make sure that society is not disrupted by drug taking. They penalize drug users and impose even harsher penalties on those who supply and profit from illegal drugs – the traffickers.

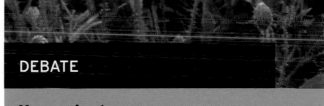

DEBATE

You are in charge

You are an outstanding sports player, greatly admired by young people. You are invited to take part in an anti-drugs TV campaign. Do you:

■ refuse, perhaps because you fear that young people will see you as a lecturing adult instead of a hero?

■ accept, and be ready to speak out about drugs in general?

■ accept, but insist on talking mainly about drugs in sport?

CHAPTER 2

Trafficking Across Frontiers

It is 2025. Rosalia Romero is a poor farmer's daughter, just 13 years old. Civil wars and violent changes of government have wrecked the South American country in which she lives. The poor are poorer than ever and must do whatever they can to survive. Soldiers have swooped on the Romeros' farm. They have arrested Rosalia's father and brothers and have destroyed their illegal coca crop, which outsiders buy and use to make cocaine. Rosalia's mother is too upset to think about the future, and Rosalia wonders how they will avoid starving. All they can do is grow something – but what? Rosalia would like to be respectable and grow oranges or coffee, but they bring in hardly any money. She tells her mother that they have no choice. They must grow a new coca crop and hope the soldiers will stay away.

Government action

Most countries have made laws that penalize people who produce, supply or use illegal drugs. But drug trafficking is not just a national problem – it is international, because many of the drugs are smuggled from country to country. A nation's customs officers, often assisted by police, will try to locate any drugs that are being smuggled across its borders. The customs service will confiscate the drugs and arrest the offenders. It will work closely with other police forces and customs services, and with international organizations such as the United Nations and the international police agency, Interpol.

A global business

Both national and international agencies face formidable problems. Huge profits can be made from international drug trafficking. That means traffickers can afford to organize their operations thoroughly and can still prosper if the authorities seize large quantities of their smuggled drugs. Many of the drugs they handle are transported across continents to reach profitable markets in wealthy parts of the world such as North America, Europe and Australia.

THE PRESIDENT'S LIST

Every year the US president sends a list of countries to Congress. They are countries identified as major producers of illegal drugs or major drug-transit countries (that is, countries through which drugs pass). In September 2008 President George W Bush named the following countries as 'majors':

- Afghanistan
- The Bahamas
- Bolivia
- Brazil
- Burma
- Colombia
- Dominican Republic
- Ecuador
- Guatemala
- Haiti
- India
- Jamaica
- Laos
- Mexico
- Nigeria
- Pakistan
- Panama
- Paraguay
- Peru
- Venezuela

A drugs bust. At Buenaventura in Colombia, policemen carry packs of cocaine, part of an almost 3,000-kilogram haul that they have just seized. If they had not acted, the drugs would have been smuggled into Mexico, probably bound for the United States.

COCAINE AND CRACK

Cocaine was developed in the mid-19th century. Its main ingredient is a substance extracted from the leaves of the South American coca plant. For thousands of years, South American mountain peoples chewed dried coca leaves, which acted as a mild stimulant. Cocaine is very much more powerful. It is usually sold as a white powder and is commonly snorted (sniffed). Crack, a relatively recent form of cocaine, is usually smoked. It creates even more violent mood swings. Cocaine and crack are highly addictive. Both carry serious health risks for users. Heavy use of crack, for example, can cause mental illness.

A Peruvian farmer chews a coca leaf. Coca has long been used by people in the mountainous regions of South America. It is a mild stimulant – unlike the hard drugs cocaine and crack, processed from the leaf.

14

Smuggling heroin and cocaine

Heroin comes from opium poppies grown in Afghanistan and other Asian countries. In South American countries such as Colombia and Bolivia, coca leaves are processed to make cocaine and crack. Typically, cocaine is smuggled from Colombia into the United States via Mexico, and into European countries via West Africa.

The growers of opium poppies and coca plants are not hardened criminals. They are mostly poor farmers who struggle to survive. They are not paid large amounts of money for their crops, although the drugs made from them will eventually command high prices on city streets. The farmers would probably prefer to grow legal crops, but only the traffickers will pay prices that enable them to survive.

CANNABIS

Cannabis, or marijuana, is used by almost 160 million people and is the most popular illicit (illegal) drug in the world. It is grown in at least 172 countries and sold in the form of leaves or a dark dried resin called hashish. Cannabis is most commonly smoked, but it may also be eaten in a cake or biscuit. Except in its very strongest form, the drug has a relaxing effect, rendering users dreamy and inactive. Cannabis is widely seen as a 'soft', relatively harmless drug, though using it may have long-term effects on the brain. The US government regards it as a 'gateway' drug, leading users on to harder drugs, but some US states accept that it has medical uses.

Smuggling cannabis

Unlike heroin and cocaine, cannabis can be grown in many parts of the world. Cannabis leaves are bulkier than drugs made in powder form, but nevertheless they are widely smuggled. Cannabis grown illegally in the United States may be smuggled across state borders. It is also smuggled into the United States from Mexico and Canada. The long US borders are hard to police. Although large quantities of cannabis are seized every year, substantial amounts get through.

Smuggling laboratory drugs

Drugs made in the laboratory, such as amphetamines, crystal meth and LSD, are also smuggled into many states. Traffickers may set up illicit laboratories in the country where they intend to sell the drugs, avoiding the risks involved in smuggling. But many of the traffickers prefer to manufacture the drugs in countries where policing is weak or penalties are relatively light. They employ other people to do the smuggling across borders, so they are actually minimizing the risks they run.

Smuggling methods

Drug smugglers employ a variety of methods. Where there are remote areas to be crossed, or the borders are poorly policed, vehicles or planes may transport quantities of drugs with little danger of being caught. The smugglers may well be professional criminals, prepared to use violence if they meet with opposition.

The ingenuity of smugglers. A Canadian police officer displays a fake duck egg packed with heroin. The egg was part of a large consignment of heroin and ecstasy, hidden among preserved duck eggs that had been shipped from China to Canada.

LABORATORY DRUGS

The main ingredients of many drugs come from plants. Heroin, cocaine, hallucinogenic mushrooms and cannabis are all plant-based drugs, though they may be processed in a laboratory before they are sold. But there are also drugs made entirely in laboratories, using chemicals. These include powerful stimulants such as amphetamines ('speed'), ecstasy, and crystal meth (methamphetamine), a concentrated and particularly dangerous form of amphetamine that has been widely used in the United States, Australia and New Zealand since the 1990s.

The best-known laboratory-made hallucinogen is LSD (lysergic acid diethylamide), which was highly fashionable in the 1960s and 1970s. Laboratory drugs are hard for the police to trace, since they can be made close to the area where they are sold, unlike drugs that have to be smuggled across frontiers.

In areas where border controls operate more effectively, smugglers find all sorts of ingenious ways to conceal their cargoes or bluff their way through customs. For example, they use official vehicles or stow the drugs in hidden compartments in the bodywork of cars or lorries. If the smugglers succeed, they get through with large quantities of the drug. However, the risk of detection is great when well-trained security forces are on the job, backed by expert assistants such as a team of 'sniffer' dogs who can identify the drug by its smell!

Puppies or 'mules'? These puppies were rescued from a Colombian laboratory. Drug traffickers were intending to surgically implant the dogs with packets of liquid heroin and carry them into the United States.

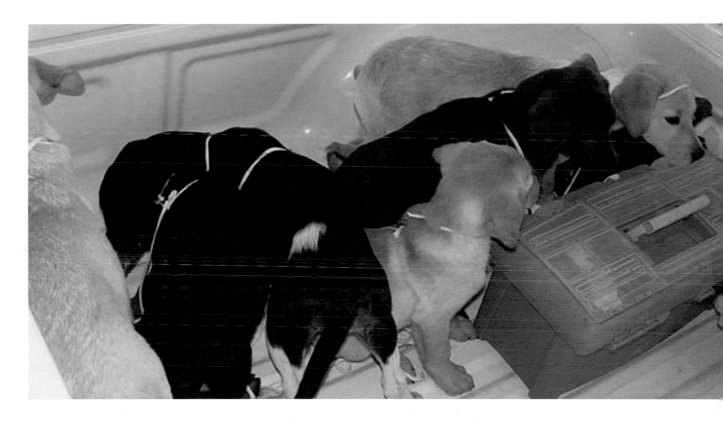

Mules

An alternative way in which smugglers operate is to use 'mules'. These are individuals who bring drugs into a country by carrying them on, or inside, their bodies. Usually the mule is not a professional criminal but an ordinary person who is desperately poor, in trouble, or foolishly tempted by the prospect of quick and easy money. Mules hope that, since they appear to be ordinary travellers or tourists, they will pass through busy customs points unchecked.

They may be carrying drugs in a pocket or backpack. A more cunning but extremely dangerous option is to swallow packets of the drugs. They are sealed in a latex or similar wrapping and carried across the border hidden in the mule's body. Authorities have become aware of this trick, however, and mules who use this method may well be caught and end up in prison. In some countries, drug mules face very harsh penalties, including the death sentence.

An even greater danger is that the wrapping will burst open. If that happens, a large quantity of the drug will be released into the mule's system, probably with fatal results. Drug trafficking across frontiers is a business in which the people at the top make fortunes and those at the bottom take the risks.

Distribution

The drugs that come onto the market in a particular country may have been produced there or may have been smuggled in from abroad. In both cases, the criminals' next step is to distribute the

Drug dealing. This dramatized photo shows a young man buying drugs from a dealer. In reality the deal would have been done much less openly, behind closed doors and with no camera present!

drugs. Large quantities are broken up into smaller amounts. These pass through the hands of a succession of traffickers. Eventually, most of the supply reaches local dealers who sell the drugs directly to the people who want to use them.

Dealers

The dealers are often themselves drug users who sell drugs to finance their own addiction, or habit. They may try to make contacts or even sell drugs on the street, looking for new customers in places such as schools and youth centres. Once they have built up regular contacts, they may start to carry out transactions in their own homes. In either case, the drug dealers' activities tend to become widely known in the local area, making it likely that the police will sooner or later trap and arrest them.

DEBATE

You are in charge

You are the leader of a country in which many farmers find it hard to make a living except by growing illegal crops for drug production. Do you:

- find the illegal crops, destroy them and arrest the farmers?

- police your country's borders more thoroughly, co-operating with neighbouring countries to stop the drugs reaching their intended market?

- encourage farmers to cultivate legal crops by, for example, starting irrigation schemes and helping them to buy seeds, fertilizers and up-to-date equipment?

- reward farmers who grow legal crops – for example by making direct payments for each legal harvest brought in, or by guaranteeing a reasonable price for legal produce?

CHAPTER 3

Drugs and Crime

It is a hot day during the summer of 2025. Josh and his friends are sitting outside the house, trying to keep cool. They talk about the vicious gang wars that are terrorizing the city. With so much money to be made from drug dealing, the gangs are constantly fighting over territory. Anybody who happens to be at the scene is likely to get hurt. While the friends are talking, a car passes, shots ring out, and the car speeds away. Two men on the other side of the street fall to the ground, bleeding. They are probably involved in gang warfare. But one of the shots has also hit a little girl who was playing nearby. When Josh and his friends reach her, she is already dead. This sort of crossfire killing happens a lot in 2025. It is unlikely even to get a mention on the TV news.

People who become drug traffickers are committing crimes, whether they make, move or sell illegal substances. In most countries, users of drugs are also breaking the law. But as well as these obvious illegalities, there are many other important links between drugs and crime.

Gangs

In a number of cities the selling of drugs has been taken over by armed gangs. In some US cities, gangs are able to dominate entire neighbourhoods, usually in the poorest areas. The power of the gangs makes it difficult for the police to investigate crimes or find witnesses brave enough to give evidence about illegal activities.

The challenge to a dominant gang is most likely to come from a rival gang. The gangs compete for territory (areas of a city they aim to control). With territory comes power, income and prestige. Vicious gang wars are fought over who rules a particular 'turf'. It is not yet 2025, but killings are already common. They often take the form of drive-by shootings in which one or more of a rival gang are mown down by gunmen from a passing car. Innocent bystanders can be, and have been, hit.

(opposite) Suspects being questioned. In a New York shopping mall, a police officer takes no chances, making the suspects rest their hands on a car bonnet so that they cannot reach for a weapon. The young men were linked with a violent drug-dealing gang. Cannabis was found in their car.

CRIMINAL PROFITS

Criminal gangs make huge profits from drug trafficking. The statistics below show the price of heroin at each stage of its journey from Asia to the United Kingdom, along with the percentage markup (the percentage increase in the price charged at each stage).

	£	markup (%)
Price per kilo paid to the farmer	450	
Price per kilo paid to Turkish handlers	8,150	1800
Price per kilo paid on entering the United Kingdom	20,500	151
Price per kilo for which the drug is sold on the street*	51,659	69

* Of course, individual sales on the street will be for much smaller amounts than a kilo.

Source: Understanding Drug Markets and How to Influence Them (Beckley Foundation Policy Programme, 2008)

Gang violence of this kind is most common in the United States, but in recent years it has begun to appear in other countries, notably South Africa. Gun crime has greatly increased in the United Kingdom and is strongly linked to drugs. In cities such as Liverpool, Birmingham and London, several people have been killed by stray bullets during battles between gangs.

Drug barons

Street dealers and gangsters take many risks. The criminals at the top of trafficking organizations make the most money and have the best chance of escaping arrest. Even when their identities are known, it is not easy to trace crimes back to these 'drug barons' and convict them for their crimes. Some drug barons, like Pablo Escobar (see page 36), are notorious gangster figures. Others prefer to remain unknown. In March 2007, police raided a Mexico City pharmaceutical company and the home of its president. The police found evidence that the company was a front for drug trafficking. The seemingly respectable president was the drug baron in charge of the operation. Police confiscated a record-breaking US$207 million, all in notes, from the president's home.

Unusual suspects

Drugs are linked to crime in other ways. The big profits to be made from drug trafficking lure some surprising people into crime. Law enforcement officers have been caught smuggling, as have business owners whose firms are doing badly. In some countries, terrorists and revolutionaries finance their activities through drug trafficking or by demanding payments from farmers who grow drug crops.

Arrest of a drug baron. Captured after a gun battle in Colombia, Luiz Fernando da Costa is seen in 2001 being taken back to his native Brazil. There, he was convicted of drug trafficking and imprisoned.

Funding a habit

Users break the law when they take drugs. But they are also likely to commit many other crimes. Most people who become heavy, regular users are just not rich enough to afford all the drugs they use. They commit crimes to find the money to fund their drug habits, or because drug use has kept them so poor that they steal in order to live. In one British survey, nine out of ten heroin and crack users claimed that they had committed crimes to pay for their drugs. Shoplifting, burglary, mugging and car theft are typical drug-related crimes. Some commit offences while under the influence of drugs – for example people who drive while on drugs often cause accidents. Statistics show that a remarkably high percentage of people in prison have been sent there for offences linked with drugs. In this and many other ways, drugs are an immense burden on society.

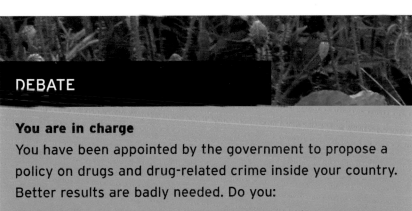

DEBATE

You are in charge

You have been appointed by the government to propose a policy on drugs and drug-related crime inside your country. Better results are badly needed. Do you:

■ press for more resources and greater police powers to search premises and arrest and hold suspects?

■ use available resources to target the most dangerous, 'hard' drugs, rather than 'soft' ones?

■ promote educational programmes that highlight the dangers and drawbacks of drug use?

■ improve programmes to rehabilitate addicts (that is, help them to end their addiction and adjust to living normal lives)?

■ allow addicts who commit crimes to join rehabilitation programmes instead of sending them to prison?

CHAPTER 4

The Social Cost

It is 2025. Natasha is a Russian woman. Because of her drug addiction, she has behaved recklessly. She has contracted hepatitis C from sharing the needles of hypodermic syringes with fellow addicts. She now realizes that drug use is ruining her life. But in 2025 the hospital system can no longer cope with the burden of rising addiction levels. Natasha has no prospect of early treatment for her addiction, or even for the disease that is damaging her liver. She tries to stop taking drugs. But she has long ago lost touch with her family, who might have supported her efforts. All her friends are drug users. It seems unlikely that she will be strong enough to turn her life around.

Damaged lives

Drug trafficking and illegal drug use have harmful effects on society at many levels. The impact on the users is obvious. Heavy users and addicts are almost certain to be unhealthy and to have shorter lives than non-users. If they are young, they may fail to complete their studies. They often lose their jobs and they are unlikely to make the best of their talents or achieve their career goals. They frequently damage or destroy their relationships with the people closest to them – their parents, husband or wife, children, friends and work colleagues. If their need for drugs drives them to crime, they will probably end up in prison or even dead.

A drug addict smokes crack in a run-down house in Managua, the capital of Nicaragua. Drug problems damage countries and people, whether they are rich or poor. Drugs have fuelled gang violence and wars in Central America.

Family breakdown

Many non-users also suffer. Family and friends often do their best to help someone with a drug problem to overcome it. A user may become violent or steal from his or her family in order to buy drugs. Even if this does not happen, the user's mood swings and erratic lifestyle put terrible strains on relationships and the family often breaks up. Its members are left devastated and sometimes never completely get over what has happened. The user leaves them, losing contact with everybody and moving mainly among fellow users, making it unlikely that he or she will ever break the drug habit.

THE MOST DANGEROUS DRUGS

Research published in the British medical journal *The Lancet* in 2007 listed the most dangerous drugs. The ratings are based on harm to the user, likelihood of becoming addicted and harm to society. Starting with the worst, the first 12 out of 20 were:

1. heroin	
2. cocaine	
3. barbiturates	a range of drugs with powerfully depressant effects
4. street methadone	used to treat drug addiction, but also sold on the street as an illegal drug
5. alcohol	
6. ketamine	a powerful depressant that causes loss of body sensation
7. benzodiazepines	used to treat drug highs that get out of hand; but highly addictive
8. amphetamines	
9. tobacco	
10. buprenorphine	a painkiller abused by drug takers
11. cannabis	
12. solvents	

Two legal drugs are high on the list: **alcohol** (no. 5) and **tobacco** (no. 9). Some well-known illegal drugs came lower down the list, notably **LSD** (no. 14) and **ecstasy** (no. 18).

Damage to society

Illegal drugs affect the lives of individuals, but they also have a powerful effect on society as a whole. Governments spend huge sums trying to suppress drug taking and trafficking. Dealing with the health and social problems caused by drugs is also a major expense. Agencies, such as social services, become involved when drug users cannot cope with everyday life or when their families or children need to be helped or taken into care. Governments pay for these 'social costs' of drugs with citizens' taxes. Experts in various countries have estimated the social costs of illegal drugs at billions of dollars.

SOCIAL COSTS OF ILLEGAL DRUGS

These are some recent estimates of the total social cost to some nations of illegal drugs. All figures are in billions of US dollars.

Country	Year	Amount
United States	2002	180.9
United Kingdom	2008	28.4
Canada	2002	8.2
Australia	2005	8.1
New Zealand	2006	1.3

Sources: The Economic Costs of Drug Abuse in the United States 1992-2002 (2004); The Financial Cost of Addiction (Addaction, 2008); The Cost of Substance Abuse in Canada 2002 (2006); The Costs of Tobacco, Alcohol and Illicit Drug Abuse to Australian Society in 2004/5; research by Business and Economic Research Ltd for the New Zealand Police (2008)

The cost of crime

For most countries, crime is the largest of all social costs. The high number of drug-related crimes mean that governments must spend very large sums on law enforcement, the justice system, prisons and the large numbers of people and institutions linked with them. In 2007, there were 1.8 million arrests in the United States for drug offences. At the end of 2004, as many as 249,000 people were in prison for such offences.

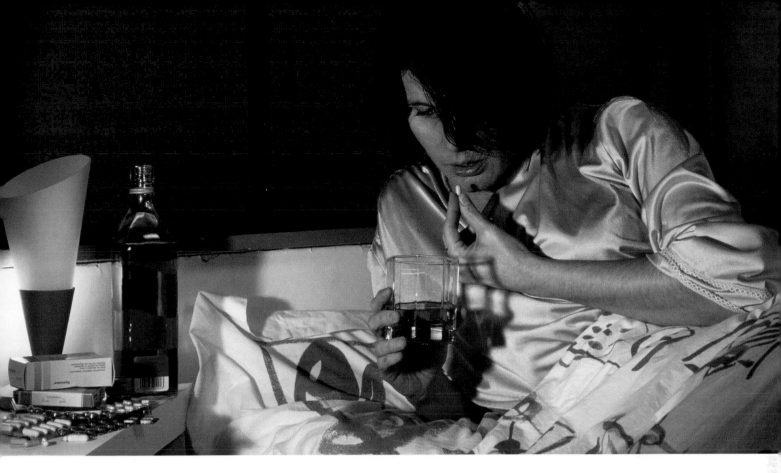

Health costs

The health costs of drug use are also substantial. Health services must:

- deal with emergencies caused by drug overdoses and drug-related accidents
- provide treatment for a range of illnesses associated with drug use, including mental problems
- offer expensive medical drugs to treat infections spread by sharing needles
- cater for the special health needs of pregnant addicts and their babies
- operate programmes to help addicts to become 'clean'

Needles and disease

Many addicts inject drugs like heroin straight into their veins, using hypodermic syringes. Not being medically trained, they may well damage themselves or contract infections such as blood poisoning. An even more dangerous practice is for several users to share the same needle. Any infection in one user's blood will be passed on to the others.

Prescription drug abuse. Some people use legally prescribed drugs to get high, but that doesn't make the pills any less dangerous than illegal drugs. This kind of drug abuse is a growing problem. In this dramatized photograph, a woman is taking pills with alcohol, a potentially deadly combination.

Very serious diseases, such as human immunodeficiency virus (HIV) and hepatitis C, can be caught in this way. Hepatitis C attacks the liver and can kill. The HIV virus destroys the immune system, which protects the body against infections. As a result, HIV can lead on to acquired immunodeficiency syndrome (AIDS), a life-threatening condition. HIV is most commonly contracted through sexual activity, but needle-sharing has claimed many additional victims.

Economic costs

In addition to these huge social expenses, there are costs to the economy and the world of work. These costs are hard to calculate because they mostly take the form of lost income or efficiency. Heavy drug users tend to make unreliable and unhealthy workers, so the enterprises they serve will be less productive than they should be. The users' health problems will cause them to be sick and absent more often than non-users doing similar jobs.

This young drug addict in Kiev, Ukraine, is preparing to inject herself. Like many people who inject drugs, she became HIV-positive through sharing needles. Given help, she stopped sharing and began to distribute clean needles and syringes to other users to try to prevent the spread of disease.

28

If users become desperate for money to finance their drug taking, they may steal from their employers or their fellow workers. Such thefts create an atmosphere of general distrust until the culprit is discovered, and may have long-lasting effects on work relationships. Whether the users are sick, inefficient or commit crimes, they will probably lose their jobs and will find it harder and harder to get new ones. Instead of contributing to society, they will become a burden on it.

All resources are limited. The money spent on drug-related crime, health and work problems cannot be spent on other things. These problems cost society billions of pounds, dollars and euros. Society's response has been to declare a 'War on Drugs' – an attempt to stamp out drug use and drug trafficking.

DEBATE

You are in charge

You are a leading figure in the health service of a European country. More and more cases of a serious disease are appearing and it is hard to find the time and resources to treat everyone. The disease can be caught in various ways, but some sufferers have contracted it through drug use, by sharing the needles with which they inject themselves. Since resources are so limited, a number of experts argue that the drug users are to blame for their condition and that non-users should always be treated first. Will you:

■ keep drug users at the back of the queue?

■ refuse to treat them unless they stop using drugs and remain 'clean' for a fixed period?

■ continue the traditional policy of seeing patients on a first-come first-served basis, except for emergency cases?

CHAPTER 5

Fighting the Traffickers

Charlie is a border guard in the year 2025. He belongs to a unit that races to trouble spots to stop people from entering the country illegally. But the task has become almost impossible. The borders are being crossed all along their length. Many of the intruders are criminals carrying illegal drugs. Neighbouring countries are close to collapse and can do nothing about the trafficking. Because it is so profitable, the traffickers are able to arm themselves at least as well as the border guards, whose job has become increasingly dangerous. Charlie is a brave man, but he worries about what will become of his wife and children if he is killed. Then the news breaks. A heavily armed party of traffickers has been spotted 75 kilometres away, heading for the border at speed. There is no time to arrange for backup. Charlie and the rest of the unit prepare to do battle.

Changing attitudes

Drug use has a long history, but laws against using drugs are comparatively recent. During the 19th century, drugs were freely available in countries like Britain and the United States. Opium was widely used as a painkiller and could be bought over the counter in pharmacies. Laudanum, a liquid form of the drug (mixed with alcohol), was especially popular. A number of people, including some famous writers, began taking laudanum as medicine and eventually became addicted to it.

Nineteenth-century chemists made many discoveries that led to the manufacture of stronger drugs. Opium was developed into morphine (1803), and morphine into heroin (1898). In 1874, cocaine was extracted from coca leaves. At first these were hailed as great scientific achievements. For a time cocaine was even used as an ingredient in Coca-Cola. Later, scientists became aware that drugs like heroin and cocaine were unsuitable for medical use and that the supply of even medically beneficial drugs like morphine needed to be controlled.

CHINA AND OPIUM

During the 19th century, China developed a serious drugs problem. Opium consumption increased steeply as supplies of the drug arrived from India, which was then under British rule. When China tried to ban opium, the British fought two wars (1839-42 and 1856-60) that forced the Chinese government to allow opium into the country. Later, Chinese immigrants brought the habit to countries like the United Kingdom and the United States. The opium dens in which they smoked the drug gained a bad reputation. Previously the victims of the opium trade, the Chinese were now blamed for bringing it to the West.

A 1925 photograph of drug users in an opium den in Chinatown, the part of New York where most Chinese then lived. Images like this one fed people's prejudices and made it easy for them to believe that the Chinese were to blame for drug problems.

Anti-drug legislation

Fear and concern about Chinese opium dens (see panel on page 31) lay behind the first US anti-drug laws, which were passed by the city of San Francisco in 1875. In 1909, the United States took the first international action against the opium trade. A US-sponsored meeting led to the Hague Convention (1912), an international agreement that committed members to outlaw opium. During the same period, the United States passed the first federal (central government) anti-drug law, the Harrison Narcotic Act (1914). In 1920, the British government also took action, passing the Dangerous Drugs Act.

These early measures became the basis for many later national and international laws and agreements. Lists of illegal drugs became steadily longer as their dangers were realized. However, in some cases this recognition came surprisingly late. Amphetamines, though manufactured since 1887, were still frequently issued to troops during World War II (1939–1945) to combat battle fatigue. Amphetamines only became illegal in the United States and the United Kingdom in the mid-1960s. Similarly, ecstasy was freely available until the mid-1980s.

Early alarms over cocaine and heroin gave way to other concerns. For a long time, attention in the United States focused on alcohol, which was an illegal drug from 1919 until 1933 (the Prohibition era). Then the emphasis shifted to marijuana, which Congress effectively outlawed in 1937 and penalized increasingly harshly in the 1950s. In the United States the drug was, and is, regarded as being as bad as cocaine and heroin.

In the 1960s, drug taking became an important part of the 'youth culture' that developed in the United States, the United Kingdom and many other countries. Governments grew alarmed enough

PROHIBITION

In 1920, whisky, beer and all other alcoholic drinks were banned in the United States. This episode in American history is generally known as Prohibition. Millions of Americans still wanted to drink, so the import, manufacture and sale of liquor was taken over by criminals. Huge profits were at stake and vicious gang wars broke out for control of the trade. Corruption was widespread, including bribery of police officers. Ordinary people became law-breakers, buying from dealers or visiting speakeasies (undercover clubs that sold drinks). A failure, Prohibition ended in 1933.

An image from 1968. With his face paint, mock uniform and wide grin, this man conveys the carefree spirit of many young people in the 1960s. The painted card on his hat reads 'LSD' - the name of the most popular hallucinogenic drug of the period.

to introduce new anti-drug laws. The United Kingdom passed the Misuse of Drugs Act (1971), which combined and updated earlier laws.

Controlled Substances Act

In the United States, the Controlled Substances Act (1970) became the basis for all later policy. The Act grouped drugs into five 'schedules', according to how likely they were to be abused and how medicinally useful they were. Most countries now operate a similar system. The Controlled Substances Act also created new federal agencies to combat drug use and trafficking. From this time, the federal (as opposed to the state and local) authorities took on a far greater role in the fight against drugs.

The War on Drugs

In June 1971, US President Richard Nixon made a speech in which he described substance abuse (taking illegal drugs) as 'public enemy number one in the United States'. He famously declared that America would wage a 'War on Drugs'.

The United States pursued the War on Drugs relentlessly. Other countries fought their own 'wars', but the US effort was the most far-reaching and spectacular. With its long borders and large, affluent population, the United States was the most tempting target for traffickers, and waging the war was hugely expensive.

As well as tough policing at home, on the borders and on the high seas, the US government took action abroad to cut off supplies from countries where drugs were produced or 'transit countries' through which drugs were transported. The United States adopted a policy of co-operating with the governments of such countries, providing funds, advisers and even special forces to help with law enforcement. Most of this activity was directed at the opium-producing regions of Central and South-East Asia and the coca-growing areas of South America.

Fighting the opium producers

In the 1990s, most of the world's opium was grown in two areas. The Central Asian 'Golden Crescent' (Afghanistan, Pakistan, Iran) had a formidable rival in the South-East Asian 'Golden Triangle', a remote, mountainous area on the borders of Myanmar, Laos and Thailand.

By the early 2000s, the Golden Triangle governments, with help from the United States, had largely stamped out opium production and trafficking. This was one of the great success stories of the War

NARCOTERRORISM

Narcoterrorism is a term used to describe terrorism funded by growing or dealing in drugs. In 2001, the United States and its allies overthrew the Taliban regime in Afghanistan, which sheltered terrorists. The Taliban have continued to resist, and finance their struggle by forcing farmers in the areas they control to produce opium. The Taliban make millions of dollars from the opium trade.

In Colombia, too, terrorists exploit the drugs trade. Groups with different political ideas have fought one another and the government for over 40 years. Several of the groups are thought to be involved in trafficking cocaine, notably FARC (Revolutionary Armed Forces of Colombia), which has carried out many kidnappings and other terrorist acts.

on Drugs. But with the loss of competition from the east, opium cultivation in Afghanistan increased rapidly. By 2008, Afghanistan produced 90 per cent of the world supply, amounting to 8,000 tonnes of opium a year.

War on drugs. An armed police guard stands by while a tractor uproots a poppy field in Afghanistan, the source of most of the world's supply of heroin.

Fighting the cocaine producers

In South America, the War on Drugs proved even harder to win. Farmers grew coca leaves in the mountainous regions of Colombia, Peru and Bolivia. They then sold them to traffickers who processed them into cocaine and smuggled the drug into the United States and other countries. The United States became involved in counter-narcotics activities in all three countries, funding and training Colombian government forces and assisting them in destroying coca crops.

PABLO ESCOBAR

The most famous of all drug barons, Pablo Escobar (1949–1993), was born in Rionegro, Colombia. At first a petty criminal, he became a dealer in cocaine. Escobar created an organization known as the Medellín Cartel, after his base, the Colombian city of Medellín. Escobar owed much of his success to his utter ruthlessness. Anyone who could not be bribed was murdered, including large numbers of judicial and police officials. The cartel smuggled vast quantities of drugs into the United States and other countries. By 1989, Escobar was reckoned to be the seventh richest man in the world. But his operations made him a target for rival gangs and Colombian and US forces. In 1993, they tracked him down and killed him in a shoot-out at his Medellín hideout.

Pablo Escobar in 1989. As the head of the Medellín drugs cartel in his native Colombia, Escobar became one of the richest and most feared men in the world. He was finally betrayed by rivals and killed in a gun battle in 1993.

During the 1970s and 1980s, the South American drugs trade was dominated by Colombian cartels (criminal organizations), which became enormously powerful and violent. The US-backed government forces began to make real progress in 1993, when Pablo Escobar, head of the notorious Medellín Cartel, was shot dead. Within two years, other leaders of the Colombian cartels had been killed, sent to prison or extradited (sent to stand trial in another country – in this case, the United States).

This was a significant victory, but it did not end the war. The traffickers reorganized and Mexican cartels took over important parts of the trade. When crops were destroyed in one area, the traffickers made use of growers in a different place or even a different country. The poverty of farmers and the huge profits of trafficking meant that the drugs trade seemed able to recover from quite devastating blows. The War on Drugs continued to have its ups and downs into the 2000s.

DEBATE

You are in charge

You are the leader of a powerful country with serious drugs problems. A very dangerous drug is produced in a country where the government is not really in control. It is willing to accept your help and stamp out drug production. Unfortunately the government has a record of illegal violence and mistreatment of opponents. Do you:

- refuse to help?
- agree to fund the training of government forces and advise on strategy, but refuse to supply weapons and insist that the government publicly commit to improving its human rights record?
- argue that what the government does inside its own territory is no business of yours, as long as it carries out its promises on drugs?

CHAPTER 6

Looking Ahead

It is 2025. Bruno is a doctor in Central Europe. He works in a clinic that treats people with drug problems. It is a very busy place, but well equipped and well funded. Thanks to improved medication and better counselling, getting over addiction is less stressful than it used to be. People must still want to give up drugs, but they have good reasons for doing so. It has become hard to get hold of illegal drugs, and consequently they have become very expensive. A series of international agreements have made smuggling across borders very risky. Law enforcement agencies inside countries use very advanced technology and have high success rates. With drug supplies running so low, using them and possibly becoming an addict seems like a bad idea. Drugs are no longer seen as cool by young people, who have become remarkably well informed. Bruno thinks of his children Magda and Peter. He realizes that they are more aware of drug dangers than he had been at their age. He feels pretty optimistic about the future.

Reports of progress

Recent reports on drug trafficking have been optimistic. The United Nations Office on Drugs and Crime (UNODC) issued a World Drug Report in 2007. It claimed that the 25-year-long rise in drug use had been halted, though worries remained about Afghanistan's soaring opium production. The United States' National Drug Threat Assessment for 2008 was similarly upbeat. Record drug seizures and strikes against traffickers had led to cocaine shortages in many cities. Methamphetamine production within the United States had fallen since 2004.

Some researchers disputed aspects of these claims. But on the whole it seemed that the situation had stabilized in the main markets (North America, Europe, Australia and New Zealand). On the other hand, reports suggested that drug use was increasing in producer countries like Afghanistan, and also in transit regions such as Western Asia and West Africa.

So the War on Drugs has not yet been won. And although stabilizing supply and use may be an achievement, existing problems are serious enough. The 2007 National Survey on Drug Use and Health estimated that 19.9 million Americans had used illegal drugs within the past month. This represented 8 per cent of Americans over the age of 11.

Iranian drug users prepare a heroin injection. Iran is a strict Islamic Republic, yet there are increasing numbers of drug users. Drugs have taken hold in Iran, as in other countries on trafficking routes to the West.

WORLDWIDE SEIZURES OF SOME ILLICIT DRUGS (IN KILOGRAMMES)

	1999	2000	2001	2002	2003	2004	2005
Heroin	36,229	53,747	54,080	48,538	53,242	60,200	58,600
Cocaine	367,898	342,441	373,106	371,551	498,941	579,400	752,300
Cannabis (resin and herb)	4,042,381	4,674,274	4,857,271	4,744,793	5,850,276	6,189,348	8,618,000

Source: United Nations Office on Drugs and Crime, World Drug Reports, 2006 and 2007

International cooperation

The War on Drugs continues to be finely balanced because advances are so often matched by setbacks. Countries improve their methods of scanning and detection and work more closely with their fellow-states. In May 2008, Iran, Pakistan and Afghanistan agreed to strengthen border co-operation to stem the flow of drugs from Afghanistan. And in June 2008, the Merida Initiative committed the United States to spend US$1.4 billion helping Mexico in matters such as law enforcement, training and equipment.

Border problems

However, the traffickers can also call on new resources. They cross the US border, from north or south, in small private planes. Recently, Colombian traffickers have even used submarines. Border controls have been improved in places, but the ever-increasing amount of traffic makes efficient checking very difficult. In Europe, goods and people pass more or less freely across borders within the 27-member European Union. As a result, problems of control have also become more complicated there.

Prevention and treatment

Most countries continue to fight against drug trafficking – the 'supply' side of the trade. But recently there has been much more emphasis on prevention and treatment, championed by, among others, the United Nations.

The policy reflects a belief that reducing the demand for drugs will benefit both individuals and society. Drug trafficking is so profitable that when one dealer is arrested, another dealer takes over the business. But if users stop wanting to buy drugs, the entire trade would collapse. Therefore some governments are focusing on reducing demand by helping people to overcome their addiction.

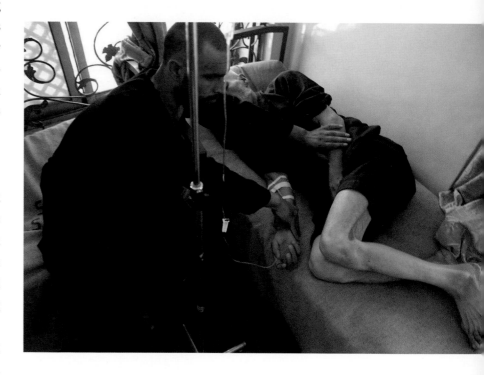

Giving up drugs is hard. A former user comforts a heroin addict who has stopped injecting and is now suffering from very painful withdrawal symptoms.

British studies suggest that a relatively small number of addicts commit a high proportion of all money-related crimes. When users were directed into treatment, there was a dramatic fall in the number of crimes they committed. Experts claimed that this was responsible for the 55 per cent fall in theft in the United Kingdom between 1997 and 2007.

In the United States, too, more attention has been given to prevention and treatment, including funding for education programmes in schools. But statistics show that US spending on tough action against users, dealers and international traffickers was still increasing. In fact, it was growing at a much faster rate than spending on prevention and treatment (see the chart below). The development of special drug courts from 1989 did, however, signal a willingness to understand and deal with individual offenders in a more focused way.

This chart compares the US government's spending on the War on Drugs with its spending on drug treatment and prevention. The chart covers the period between 2002 and 2008.

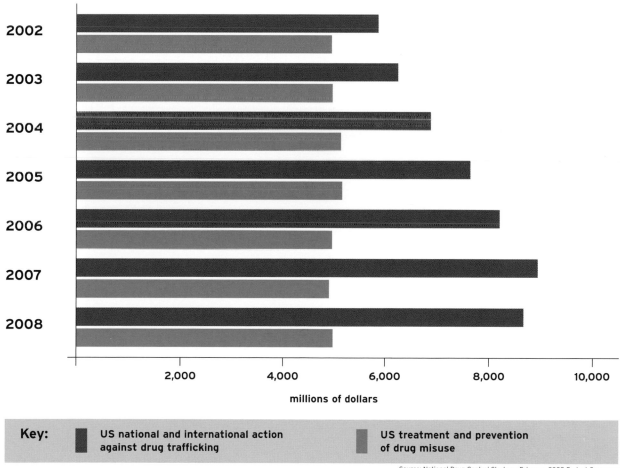

millions of dollars

Key:

■ **US national and international action against drug trafficking**

■ **US treatment and prevention of drug misuse**

Source: National Drug Control Strategy, February 2009 Budget Summary

Harm reduction

The United Nations (UN) is among the organizations that favour a principle known as harm reduction. This means trying to limit the damage done to and by users. For example, addicts' use of shared needles may spread diseases, and the infection may be passed on to non-addicts. The principle of harm reduction has led to some surprising initiatives. In 2001, Australia began to introduce injecting rooms, where addicts could obtain and use clean needles. In 2005, addicts in certain Canadian cities were issued with limited supplies of heroin to keep them out of trouble. Critics have denounced such experiments, arguing that they make drug users feel that what they are doing is acceptable.

Different approaches

There are other important differences between the way nations approach drug issues. The United States is notably tough on those who use drugs as well as those who deal in them. Penalties vary according to circumstances, but are generally severe. The United States classifies drugs into five schedules (groups). Schedule 1 drugs are those that are highly likely to be abused and are considered to

Australia's first injecting room just after it opened in 2001. The medical director stands in the new facility, where addicts can inject in hygienic conditions.

have no medical use. They include heroin, LSD, cannabis and ecstasy. Schedule 2 drugs, such as cocaine, methamphetamine, amphetamines and morphine, are also liable to abuse but have limited medical uses. Schedule 3 drugs, which include barbiturates and steroids, have less potential for abuse and more widely accepted medical uses.

The British approach is broadly similar to that of the United States, though its classification system is slightly different (see panel).

CLASSIFIED DRUGS IN THE UNITED KINGDOM

In the United Kingdom, drugs are officially grouped into three classes: A, B and C. The classification reflects the harm that experts believe the drug can do. The most severe penalties are reserved for the most harmful, Class A drugs. As in most countries, dealing is more severely punished than possession or use of drugs.

Class	Some classified drugs	Penalties for possession	Penalties for dealing
A	heroin, cocaine, crack, LSD, ecstasy, crystal meth, magic mushrooms	up to 7 years in prison or unlimited fine; or both	up to life in prison or unlimited fine; or both
B	amphetamines, cannabis*, Ritalin	up to 5 years in prison or unlimited fine; or both	up to 14 years in prison or unlimited fine; or both
C	tranquillizers, ketamine, some painkillers	up to 2 years in prison	up to 14 years in prison or unlimited fine; or both

*reclassified from C to B from 2009

Source: Home Office www.homeoffice.gov.uk/drugs/drugs-law/

A number of European countries have a different approach. Portugal punishes drug dealing, but since 2001 it has treated drug use and addiction as medical problems rather than crimes. When a user is found in possession of drugs, they are confiscated. He, or she, is examined by a health and welfare commission, which decides on appropriate treatment.

DRUG EPIDEMIC

From the 1990s, a little-known drug became disturbingly popular in the United States, Australia and New Zealand. Methamphetamine, a concentrated and dangerous form of amphetamine, is better known as crystal meth. Anyone smoking crystal meth experiences an intense high, four times stronger than the high from cocaine. But the payback, in terms of exhaustion, addiction and mental deterioration, is equally extreme and happens quickly. An important ingredient of crystal meth is pseudophedrine, which is found in a number of medicines. The United States' 2005 Combat Methamphetamine Epidemic Act allowed people to buy pseudophedrine only after the closest of checks. By 2007, the British authorities had also become concerned about increasing use of crystal meth, and they changed its status to a Class A drug.

The child in this photograph is being cuddled by his new sister. He has been adopted by a kindly family after being neglected by his own parents, who were crystal meth addicts. Such children often have serious health problems.

Decriminalizing cannabis

Many countries have laws against possessing cannabis but do not enforce them very vigorously. The drug is widely thought of as 'soft', with less serious immediate effects than heroin and cocaine. This is one reason why Belgium and Switzerland have decided not to regard possession of cannabis as a crime. Users who possess small amounts are not interfered with.

The Netherlands has launched the most radical policy experiment so far. The policy strongly emphasizes harm reduction. Possessing small amounts of cannabis for personal use is not a criminal offence. And, most controversially, hundreds of adult-only cafés sell small amounts (5 grammes) of cannabis, which users can smoke on the premises. The Dutch scheme has been widely criticized by European neighbours and others, who believe that treating cannabis smoking as an ordinary, everyday activity is misguided.

Changing attitudes

Even in Europe, the trend is not all in one direction. Governments change, and policies change with them. In 2006, a recently elected Italian government introduced laws that replaced a mild attitude towards drug possession with very stiff penalties. Political pressures, new evidence, new treatments and new strains of known drugs can all affect government policies.

The existence of different approaches to drug problems has its advantages. Over time, some policies should show better results than others. If they do, governments will gradually adopt them and further progress can be expected. A world free of illegal drugs may be a distant dream. But it should be possible to create a world in which drugs no longer ruin thousands of lives and threaten the health of societies.

DEBATE

You are in charge

You are a school head. Your school has never had any serious trouble with drugs, but now there are rumours that a student is dealing drugs on the premises. Do you:

- employ someone to search students as they come into school?
- ask the government or health authorities to start testing students for evidence of drug taking?
- start a counselling service within the school to help young people who are tempted by drugs or have drug problems of any kind?
- put up posters telling students about telephone helplines where they can ask for advice or give information about drug dealing without their own names becoming known?

Glossary

addiction A condition in which a person finds it almost impossible to stop using a drug, even when it is obviously harming him or her.

AIDS See HIV/AIDS.

bust A police arrest, especially one that nets many criminals and breaks up their organization.

caffeine The drug present in coffee, tea, chocolate and many soft drinks.

coca The South American plant from which cocaine is made.

dealer A person who sells drugs.

dependence Another word for addiction.

drug baron A top criminal who runs a drug-dealing network.

extradite When a person is extradited, he or she is removed from a country, with the permission of that country's government, to stand trial in a different country. This is possible through an extradition treaty between the countries concerned.

'gateway' drug A 'soft' drug whose use is believed by some people to lead on to the use of more harmful, 'hard' drugs.

hallucinogen A drug that distorts the user's sense of reality, producing hallucinations.

hard drug A drug that has visibly serious, negative effects on users.

hepatitis C A disease of the liver.

HIV/AIDS HIV (human immunodeficiency virus) is a virus that destroys the immune system that protects against infections. People whose infections resulting from HIV have become life-threatening are described as having AIDS (acquired immunodeficiency syndrome).

hypodermic syringe A medical instrument for giving injections, also employed by drug users.

mule A person paid to carry drugs through checkpoints on national frontiers.

narcoterrorism Literally 'drug terrorism': terrorism funded by the profits from growing or dealing in drugs.

narcotics Illegal drugs.

nicotine The drug in cigarettes that makes it hard for a regular smoker to stop using them.

opiate A sedative drug, made from the opium poppy. Opiates include codeine, morphine and opium.

overdose Excessive drug use that takes place on a single occasion, with life-threatening or fatal results.

peer pressure The pressure to behave like other members of a group; it tends to be very strong among young people.

pharmaceutical To do with medicines and drugs.

rehabilitation The process by which a drug user is able to become a normally functioning member of the community.

sedative A drug that makes the user relaxed or drowsy.

soft drug A drug whose effects are less obviously harmful than 'hard' drugs such as heroin.

solvent One of many products, including glue and lighter fluid, that can be used like a drug ('solvent abuse'), typically by sniffing the vapours the substance gives off.

steroids Drugs that build up the muscles and improve sporting performance.

stimulant A drug that gives the user a sense of being more alive, making him or her feel more energetic and confident.

Further Information

Books

Drugs 101: An Overview for Teens by Margaret O Hyde and John F Setaro (Twenty-First Century Books, 2003)

In the News: Drug Culture by A Smith (Franklin Watts, 2003)

Issues: Drug Abuse by Craig Donnellan (editor) (Independence Educational Publishers, 2006)

Just the Facts: The Drugs Trade by Jim McGuigan (Heinemann, 2005)

Twenty-First Century Debates: The Drugs Trade by Louie Fooks (Wayland, 2003)

Websites

teens.drugabuse.gov/
NIDA (National Institute on Drug Abuse) for teens: an official US site that provides information on how a wide range of drugs affect the brain and body.

www.talktofrank.com/home_html.aspx
A website funded by the British government, including an A-Z of drugs, information on rehabilitation and details of email, online and telephone help and information.

www.freevibe.com/
An interactive US website that investigates the risks of drug taking and includes actual young people's stories.

news.bbc.co.uk/1/hi/in_depth/uk/2005 drugs/default.stm
A regularly updated BBC website with world news about drugs and good links to other websites.

www.unodoc.org/youthnet/
The Global Youth Network: a UNODOC (United Nations Office on Drugs and Crime) website offering fact-based news about drugs topics involving young people all round the world.

Debate Panel Answers

Page 11:
You may consider refusing because some of your admirers will think you are being 'uncool'. But the issue is so important that you should definitely accept. Since you are probably not an expert on drugs, you will be taken most seriously if you stick to the area you know about. You can almost certainly speak with authority about cases of performance-enhancing drugs in sports which have come to light in recent years. You can wholeheartedly condemn this kind of drug use, which endangers health, is basically a form of cheating, and ends the careers of those who are caught.

Page 19:
If you are a good president, you will try to look after all your people. You will not want poor farmers to suffer, so you will keep direct action against them to a minimum. In any case, if only drug crops offer farmers a decent living, they will probably plant them again once the police or army have gone. Patrolling the borders and cooperating with neighbouring states will, if effective, certainly hurt the traffickers. But the only long-term solution is to make it worthwhile for farmers to stop cultivating drug crops and grow other foodstuffs. This is easier said than done. Rewarding farmers for harvesting alternative crops will make it easier for them to change, but sooner or later the new crops will have to pay for themselves. Schemes involving irrigation and fertilizers are more useful in the long run, since they improve the quality and size of the harvest.

Page 23:
These questions are well worth debating, though there are no clear-cut answers. Most people would like to see more effective policing, but increased police powers have less support. In democracies, people value their rights and want to limit the power of governments and police to interfere with them. You may approve of targeting 'hard' rather than 'soft' drugs if you accept that there are significant differences between them. Your decision may also depend on whether you believe that using 'soft' drugs leads on to the use of 'hard' ones. Few people would question the value of educational and rehabilitation programmes. And since prisons are already overcrowded, there are obvious advantages in sending offenders to 'rehab' rather than jailing them.

Page 29:
You may be tempted to concentrate resources on people whose sickness seems to be the result of bad luck, an accident or the effects of age rather than self-harming behaviour. However, not everyone would agree that all drug addicts are to blame for their condition. Even more important, any system of preferential treatment involves a number of difficulties and dangers. If drug users and smokers are penalized, why not heavy drinkers, reckless drivers, obese people, would-be suicides, people who go in for mountaineering and extreme sports, or children who cross roads carelessly? There may be no real alternative to the traditional obligation on the medical profession to treat all sick people.

Page 37:
If you are committed to action abroad against drugs, you will be reluctant to refuse to assist the foreign government altogether. Your best option is to help, but to do everything possible to prevent human rights abuses. You can make sure that advisers you send will report such abuses. And perhaps you could arrange for people from newspapers or TV to report on operations, since even brutal regimes dislike bad publicity. Most important of all, you can use your funds to give direct assistance to the farmers who grow drug crops. The regime you are helping may wipe out the crops, but if the farmers remain poor, they will probably go back to their old habits at the first opportunity. If you help farmers to prosper, they are not likely to turn to crime.

Page 45:
Your school has been trouble free, so there is a good case for moving cautiously in a rumour-based situation. Searching students and testing for drugs may well create a tense, unpleasant atmosphere. The United Kingdom and Australia have considered proposals for drug testing in schools but have rejected them. In the United States, testing is used only for out-of-school activities. You may set up some form of counselling in the school, but students are often reluctant to discuss sensitive matters in a place where they are known. Directing them to helplines must be a good idea. You might also set up a course of talks on various topics in the school, including one with information about drug dangers and the evils of dealing.

Index

Page numbers in **bold** refer to illustrations and charts.